Morning Sun
on a White Piano

Also by Dr. Robin R. Meyers

With Ears to Hear:
Preaching as Self-Persuasion
(Pilgrim Press, 1993)

Morning Sun
on a White Piano

Dr. Robin R. Meyers

Galilee
Doubleday

New York London Toronto Sydney Auckland

A GALILEE BOOK
PUBLISHED BY DOUBLEDAY
a division of Random House, Inc.
1540 Broadway, New York, New York 10036

GALILEE, DOUBLEDAY, and the portrayal of a ship with a cross above a
book are trademarks of Doubleday, a division of Random House, Inc.

Illustrations by Donna McCormack
Design by Brian Mulligan

Morning Sun on a White Piano was first published by Doubleday in
March 1998.

The Library of Congress has cataloged the Doubleday hardcover edition
as follows:

Meyers, Robin R. (Robin Rex), 1952–
Morning sun on a white piano / Robin R. Meyers.—1st ed.
p.   cm.
1. Spiritual life—Christianity. 2. Simplicity—Religious
aspects—Christianity. 3. Meyers, Robin R. (Robin Rex), 1952– .
I. Title.
BV4501.2.M467 1998   97-23082
248.4—dc21   CIP

ISBN 0-385-49869-1

10 9 8 7 6 5 4 3 2 1

To My Wife, Shawn—
Who Is Simply Beautiful

To the faculty, staff, and administration of Oklahoma City University, for giving me students to teach, and the freedom to teach them. To the beloved members of Mayflower Congregational UCC Church, for restoring my faith in organized religion. To my mother and father, for their legacy of love and language. To Bill Moyers, for his friendship and encouragement. And to Bruce Tracy at Doubleday, for believing in this book.

Contents

Morning Sun
on a White Piano

Introduction

~~~~~~~~~~

The premise of this book is that most of us are working frantically to secure the "good life," while expending the only life we have in the process. We put off living until the "living is good," only to discover that we never learned *how* to live in the first place.

There's a lot of talk these days about slowing down, simplifying, returning to Walden Pond, but I don't see it happening. Thoreau makes a great artifact for the coffee table, but in real life people seem to be moving faster and faster and enjoying their lives less and less.

Oddly, just as we seem to be on the verge of discovering a Unified Theory of Creation, we appear to be no closer to a Unified Theory of Living. While scientists are discovering the interconnectedness of everything in nature, the business of life itself still seems hopelessly fragmented: work is more punishment than vocation (Monday symbolizes tedium, while Friday stands for liberation); play is some form of indulgence that never quite satisfies; and meanwhile we pass each other in the halls, making plans for the "perfect vacation."

In short, we "serve time" in search of "real time" and never quite grasp the fact that *now* is as real as it gets. Life happens while we wait for something to happen, and so it's no wonder that when we get there nothing seems to be happening!

Our problem, now as always, is that we pass life by in search of it. We decide in advance which moments are worthwhile, and which are "ordinary," and thus we stifle the very movement of the spirit that we seek. Because we view simple things as mundane, it's no wonder that most of the time we are bored. Constantly reminded that sophisticated people do sophisticated things and simple people do simple things, we end up feeling sorry for our simple selves most of the time.

If the Beautiful People are doing decadent things in the south of France, who are we to suggest that watching the moon rise or rocking a baby is better than the party? If someone is bungee-jumping into the Royal Gorge, who are we to say that ironing a shirt, or sipping coffee, or breathing in the fragrant cheek of a child is somehow more satisfying, even if it is less thrilling?

What we need, more than anything, is not just to sing the song ("Simplify Life"), but to learn the *dance*. We need suggestions, concrete and sensible prescriptions for living the simple and sacramental life. We've heard all about how good this would be for us. Now we need to talk about how to *do* it.

This book intends to provide just such practical advice. It is both a rationale for the simple life and a menu of sorts, a dozen homilies on a dozen "lost arts" of living. It's a book about the *moment*, and about all the seemingly insignificant things occurring every day that are worthy of worship. It's about *hearing* again, in a culture that has gone deaf. It's about *seeing* again, in a culture that is blinded. It's about *feeling* again, in a culture that overstimulates and thus numbs itself.

Ever mindful that happiness is a by-product, as John Stuart Mill reminded us, this is a book about how to be happy without really trying and about how to make one's home into a temple, regardless of the decor. It is written in the hope that some of the tenderness of childhood remains in all of us, long after childish fear and cruelty have been outgrown. It's a simple book, about simple truth and the simple living that brings it to light. As the twentieth century winds down and a new millennium dawns, human beings need to move forward, but not by leaving the best of themselves behind.

~~~~~~~

I

The Lost Art
of Conversation

Expression is the one
fundamental sacrament.

—Alfred North Whitehead

Every morning, as our infant son lies cooing in his crib, we make sure that he hears his name before he sees our faces. "Cass . . . Cass Isaac," we call out in a drawn and almost forlorn tone of voice. His cooing stops. He hears a familiar sound. If we hide around the corner out of sight, his eyes grow bright, but he doesn't make a sound. Without a face to watch, all his energy goes to listening. The adults are making noises again, he thinks. Vibrations that name me, and prove that I exist, have traveled across the air from Someplace Else and into my fuzzy and not-well-focused world.

This may not sound like much, but it is the essential human transaction. We speak the world into being—it is "linguistically constituted," as Heidegger would say, because humans are *Homo loquins* (speaking animals). The whole of our civilization and sophistication depends on language. In the poetry of Genesis, God *speaks* the world into being, saying,

"Let there be light. . . ." In the prologue to John's Gospel, Jesus is the linguistic incarnation, God's best word, which "became flesh and dwelt among us full of grace and peace."

The story of the Tower of Babel is meant to show that when language fails, human communication and, therefore, cooperation are impossible. These days, the tragedy is not confusion, but silence—people moving, ghostlike, in glass houses against which no one dares to throw the stone of a word.

Consider our little boy again. He is learning not only that human beings make sounds to reach out to one another, but that a face will follow the sound—because the world is acoustical cause and effect. It's the *ear* that welcomes the footsteps of the world. The dog barks, the thunder rolls, the screen door bangs out its hyphenated greeting. Sound is a messenger, and an interpreter.

Long before our culture opted for the visual over the auditory, it was an acoustical highway that God traveled: in the ear of the prophet, in the narrative of the water well, in the ringing simplicity of the Sermon on the Mount. To live the simple, sacramental life again, we must put conversation back where it belongs: at the center of human life.

The world is full of noise, but starved for meaningful discourse. There is plenty of clatter and droning, the kind that spills from the airport P.A. and churns out insults over talk radio. But there is very little real communication. In fact, the

American home has become the noisiest place of utter silence on earth.

The reason: television has replaced the linguistic impulse. It turns faces *away* from one another and toward the mosaic monologue that is entertainment. The art of conversation began to die when we moved from the table to the couch. Passively we listened to *others* talking, and there was no place for us to speak our lines. We laughed at *other* people being funny, cried when *others* were sad, and cheered our sports heroes as if *we* were playing. As the flickering light of the tube reflected the zombie-like faces of a whole generation, the sound of families being families—arguing, teasing, cajoling, encouraging, setting and testing boundaries, investigating one another's feelings, and telling stories—faded to black.

The extent of this silence in a world of racket is so far advanced that drastic measures are needed. Love cannot survive silence. Children cannot grow apart from the words that bridge their fears, and adults cannot rehearse and refine their relationships if they never hear the sound of the voices they love "caressing the moment."

In a world where divorce is commonplace, it is no secret that marriages not only end *in* silence, they are ended *by* silence. Conversation is the currency of passion; it is the courier of concern. To be listened to, really listened to, and to be heard is so fundamental to the renewal of intimacy that it has become the desperate refrain of our time.

~~~~

What then is the first move in the recovery of a sacramental life of simple pleasures? It is to cut the cord on the television set—that cultural IV bottle that drips its anxiety and terror into the sanctity of sacred space and keeps us all drugged with impossible images of the unattainable life. It is to say by action, and not by sentiment alone, that you refuse to let yourself be shown how to *look*, how to *act*, and what to *wear*. For only when the blue light of television fades will people get to know themselves again in the white light of morning.

If you can't manage something this radical, then at least make a pledge to regard the television set as an enemy of the spirit, a seductive, anesthetizing intruder upon all that is real and rewarding about the proxemics of family life. Use it for information, and seek out its worthy offerings, but avoid allowing it to provide background noise in your house. It kills conversation. And whatever kills conversation should be arrested, detained, even permanently imprisoned.

If you can manage this, and be strict about it, a certain disconcerting silence will descend upon the house. The sound of canned laughter will vanish along with the sound of applause-on-command. The droning narcissism of sitcoms, the bullets and breaking glass of our love/hate relationship with violence, the electronic freak shows that dominate daytime TV—all hushed with the push of a button.

Silence is golden, we say. But at first it's a little bit frightening. Left to ourselves, and the fertile empty space which quietness creates, we may begin to muse, to reminisce, to anticipate our next conversation—even to have a conversation with ourselves. All reflection, in a sense, is predicated upon the embrace of emptiness. Until we have spent some time with silence, we can hardly claim that breaking it is worthwhile.

All of this requires a real change of lifestyle. At first, lack of practice will masquerade as awkwardness. You'll ask the children at the table, "How was school today?" And they will answer, "Fine." Likewise with a spouse: "How was your day?" "OK." Until the art of conversation is revived, lots of well-intentioned starts will sputter and die.

But conversation, like all the best things in life, cannot be forced. It develops best when children overhear it being practiced in ways that are genuine, probing, and spirited. At our table, the children usually join in after the parents have already talked their way down the road, and they decide not to get left behind.

As for that tired bromide "Never discuss religion and politics," one would be well advised to remember the premise that underlies it: these are important things; they deal with what Maslow calls "core values." That's why, at least at home, they should be talked about all the time. Conversation is how values get ordered, how passion is made contagious. If a *parent* talks about it, it's important. If a child is allowed to join the conversation, then that child becomes more than a table decoration, she has a part to play in the drama that is growing up. If her ideas count, then she counts. Children gain essential access to adulthood by being given a safe place to speak and by rehearing their thoughts out loud before the most patient and supportive audience they will ever know.

This then is the *first* prescription for the recovery of a sacramental life of simple pleasures: resolve to *talk* more and to be *entertained* less. If you're a parent, throw a log on the fire of conversation, and your children will inevitably migrate from their own form of solitude to join the communion they crave. Parents who complain that their kids won't talk to them are usually parents who don't talk to each other. The same is true even if you have no children. Every relationship is initiated by conversation, and every relationship is sustained by it.

"Language is the house of being," Heidegger said. If that's true, then there are mansions which have been made into shacks by silence, and there are simple dwellings that feel palatial because the sound of life is inside them. Breaking the silence is a gift that we can all give, a blessing disguised as "ordinary." Just *speak* across the chasms that divide us, for human speech is neither cheap nor small.

Wordsworth used to seed his discourse with long-lost friends by beginning this way: "Tell me, what has come clear

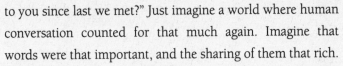

to you since last we met?" Just imagine a world where human conversation counted for that much again. Imagine that words were that important, and the sharing of them that rich.

Sometimes all we are looking for in this life is a *word* from someone. A word of reassurance, a word of forgiveness, a word of reconciliation. The authentic life is worth talking about. Talking about it makes it more authentic still. It's time to move off the couch and get back to the table—because we cannot live without the sound of each other.

~~~~

II

Music
and the
Measured Life

Music must take rank
as the highest of the fine arts —
as the one which, more than any other,
ministers to human welfare.

—*Herbert Spenser*

A few years ago, my family bought me a musical Christmas present—a triple CD retrospective of Paul Simon's life and work. It spanned the years 1964–1993, beginning with the funky and sophomoric "Leaves That Are Green" and ending with the deeply spiritual offerings of *Graceland* and *Rhythm of the Saints*. It is playing on the stereo now, as I write.

This would be an unimportant footnote, if music itself were not so important to human beings. On that Christmas Day, after the squealing and clutter of the morning had given way to the strange melancholy that is Christmas afternoon, I did something that I hadn't done since adolescence: I put on the headphones, curled up on the floor, and lived my whole life over again.

What is it about the combination of sound and poetry that

makes for such a powerful and nostalgic elixir? Does music exist because human beings are born with rhythm, wired to crave melody? Maybe so. From the measured beating of our mother's heart in the womb to the brittle waltz of an elderly couple, we *move* as a symptom of life itself. We cease to move only when we become self-conscious and fear looking foolish.

When the mystics wrote about the "music of the spheres," they were trying to dignify a mode of revelation. Music moves us because it launches us, like a boat onto a moving river. And we do not feel responsible for the destination, so much as we feel meant to enjoy the trip—especially that floating feeling that makes us seem light and sways us like the coursing of blood in our veins. Music is both an excuse not to be rational and a backdrop for the unfolding of reason itself.

The simple, sacramental life craves music the way it craves food—cooked slowly and served in courses. It anticipates the flavor of a familiar verse, a remembered melody that never fails to satisfy. One could argue that music is, practically speaking, worthless. It has no utility, produces nothing of tangible value. For all the compulsive toil that goes into making it, it remains nothing but noise—the artful interruption of silence.

Yet again, it is the life of the *ear* that is recommended here over the life of the *eye*. Every child should be taught to play a musical instrument, and it doesn't matter which one. Music

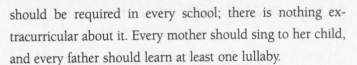

should be required in every school; there is nothing extracurricular about it. Every mother should sing to her child, and every father should learn at least one lullaby.

It is amazing to see what happens when children are taken to concerts where live music is performed. They will protest the whole idea at first, but they will be swept into the magic of it before the night is over. And they should be encouraged to dance whenever possible. The sight of children dancing unself-consciously is one of life's most beautiful things.

In fact, the simple, sacramental life has lots of dancing in it, because movement itself is such a dependable pleasure, such a symptom of joy. It's not necessary to learn how to dance; it's only necessary to become less inhibited about physical movement. Because when you think about it, lack of movement is really a form of death. Music and dancing are forms of life, swaying the soul, tapping the sweat of passion, and serving to remind the body how beautiful it is.

It also doesn't matter what kind of music you listen to. People have always used music to measure sophistication, but that's a foolish game. Every generation creates a sound that it believes is unique. The new replaces the old with an oblivious zeal. The truth is, sons trash their father's music without realizing that what they reject is the very sound their fathers used to trash the music of their grandfathers. Nothing new under the sun! Besides, all music accomplishes basically the same thing: it raises the flag of memory, it conjures the kiss, it narrates the dream. And for our purposes, it does something indispensable for the quality of life: it reminds us that cooperation and timing are everything.

Consider the orchestra as a metaphor for the very possibility of civilization. Apart from the occasional solo, most musicians have a *part* to play, and they are asked to blend in, not to upstage. To play an instrument, and to make harmony with other instruments, is more an exercise in restraint than in exuberance. Improvisation is made possible by convention— the same key, the same beat, the same intervals of rest. We play by the rules in order to break them—all creativity works this way. That's why music not only soothes "a savage breast," but reminds us that without precision and context, life is more racket than rhythm.

There is a time to whisper and a time to shout. There is a time to say nothing at all. Music teaches, by subtle example, that life is played out by measures of the appropriate and the inappropriate more often than by verdicts of right and wrong. Refrains teach the art of repetition; minor keys are bewitching; and dissonance is an artful form of discomfort.

Rhythm and crescendo are the twin virtues of lovemaking; percussion brings out the moon; flutes are flirtatious; saxophones are earthy; cellos are mournful and throaty. Music makes moods, and moods drive moments, and moments are all we have. Hence, the sacramental life calls for a kind of *emotional* virtuosity: life's occasions dictating life's sounds. Thomas Moore, author of *Care of the Soul*, reminds us that most of us need to live more rhythmically and that medieval medicine found parallels among musical rhythms, the timing of the seasons, and the tonal variations of the soul.

Technology has made it possible to carry music anywhere, but the best way to listen to music is to listen to it *live*—to go where human beings are making it, to see the faces attached to its creation, to feel the communion of friends it creates. It's a better date than the movies, a more soulful evening than any piece of video could hope to be. The eye may be the window to the soul, but the ear is closer to the heart.

Once, on a visit to Colorado Springs, I wandered into Acacia Park at lunchtime to hear old men playing jazz on an open-air bandstand, and I witnessed firsthand what live music can do to a company of strangers. First I noticed young children, too young to be inhibited about dancing, bopping and weaving in front of the stage. They were not dancing to be watched or to attract a prospective mate, but because it was in their *nature* to dance. Then I saw something wonderful. Three elderly women, all at least eighty years old, were shuffling together in a gingerly kind of chorus line. One of them was teaching the other two how it went—first this foot and then that one. The two students watched their teacher with a girlish intensity, and their bowlegs shuffled some line dance from a forgotten cabaret. I watched them for a long time and thought how remarkably like young girls they seemed, except for the gray hair. It was the sisterhood, freed up by rhythm. It was a body-memory of the way it used to be, the way it *had* to be if they were going to stay alive.

Then one of the old women picked up a young black child, an infant, and started pirouetting around the stage. They both swayed and giggled. The child's mother grabbed a camera, as if to capture this momentary reconciliation of the human race—the very young, the very old, different races— dancing. I don't know how the pictures turned out. But I know this: in one form or another, we need to sing and be sung to.

This then is the *second* prescription for the recovery of simple pleasures and the sacramental life: find the musical sound you love and, like a suitor, go to it often. Don't forget that life's most satisfying things are given to us in a moment of time and can never be duplicated no matter how much audio- or videotape we buy. Those prohibitions against taping the concert are not just legal matters; they are admissions of a deeper truth: how dare you think this moment can be carried away under your arm?

The next time you go to hear live music, consider that time before the concert, when the musicians are tuning up, to be very much like the work of the soul. It is all a noisy, cranky cacophony until joined in the service of harmony. We may do

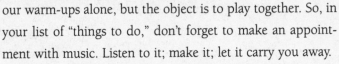

our warm-ups alone, but the object is to play together. So, in your list of "things to do," don't forget to make an appointment with music. Listen to it; make it; let it carry you away.

Music is a staple of the sacramental life. Like a river that flows from the mouth of time, music rolls on, with or without you. All you have to do is push away from the shore, and push away often—for memory and hope are the deepest of currents.

~~~~~~

Eating Books:
The Feast
of Imagination

There is no frigate like a book.

—*Emily Dickinson*

Children's books are now edible. This is a fairly recent development, and a very sensible one. With cardboard pages and rounded edges, these board books (or "chunky" books, as they're called), can be gnawed on and slobbered over in lieu of being actually read. It occurs to me that this is not only a good idea for babies, but the perfect analogy for the importance of reading in life—long after the impulse to cut teeth has faded. Because no matter what our age, we ought never to stop eating books, for books are the feast of the imagination.

At the top of the list of things to be alarmed about these days is this: too many people have stopped reading. In small towns where libraries have closed for lack of funds and patrons, the omnipresent video store stays lit well into the night. People line up with their membership cards to purchase a largely passive form of entertainment, a spectacle, the latest montage of images cut and pasted into seamless illusions requiring little more from us than occasional groping in the popcorn bowl. As for that icon of civilization, the Reading Room, where a sophisticated silence ruled (shhh!), it has become a relic of the aging library—preserved more by Christian Scientists than by culture.

Children who used to curl up with a good book to fight boredom now run electronic mazes and slay electronic dragons. Despite the assurances of former presidents that we would inherit a whole generation with excellent eye-hand coordination who would make excellent pilots, the sight of a child playing Nintendo does not compare to the sight of a child bent over a good book, traveling at warp speed through cerebral time and intellectual space.

I turn my head just now to see my sixteen-year-old son, Blue, sitting by the fireplace in the cabin reading a *Star Trek* book. It is a beautiful sight, his nearly shaved head and gold earring bent over the words on a page as he explores space, the "final frontier." Is he "beaming up" just now, or battling Klingons? Who knows? But he's reading. So is his sister, Chelsea, also lost in the creases of a book. There's no television set at the cabin, and they have forgotten that they miss it.

My wife, Shawn, the artist, sits in the rocker nearby, also reading. Her book is about parenting, a refresher course for this third-time mother. There sit the three of them, reading as I write about the importance of it. An early afternoon thunderstorm, like clockwork in the mountains, is folding down around us, and in my stupor I imagine a kind of energy humming over their heads, like the whine of high-voltage wires.

We have made our annual trek to the Chinook Book Shop in Colorado Springs, and we all have prizes in hand, each with a complimentary bookmark. Chunks of somebody else's brain, tales of somebody else's journey, portable wisdom, intimate conversations to overhear, the fossilized etchings of passion. Books with slick, beautiful covers endorsed by lots of smart people who got there before we did and are promising that we won't be disappointed. Books—they come home hot in your hands, and then by increments they warm your life, like heated bricks in a New England bed.

Let's consider just a few of the reasons why the simple and sacramental life requires books in the house. To begin with, these are *physical* artifacts; whether old or new they take up space in the house. Unlike so much in our world that is transient and brought to us on somebody else's schedule, books wait patiently to be taken up when the time is right. They gather dust and turn yellow, to be sure, but they do not disappear. They are a kind of kinetic energy under cover, promises on the spine, blood turned into ink which, when read, turns back into blood.

Books can also bring the dead back to life, and thereby make thoughts immortal. By outliving their authors, books guarantee that truth doesn't have to be reinvented by each generation. Sadly, those who never read are crippled by the deadly fiction that nothing of much importance occurred before their lifetime. Such people are "intellectual orphans," and their numbers are growing.

What's more, books create a kind of unspoken *communion*, safely bringing strangers into the house without having to worry about where they will sleep. They preserve order and teach anticipation, beginning with the introduction and holding us fast until the final period. All this is to say that one can have a *relationship* with books, a relationship that the reader can shape and control.

Unlike so many of the experiences that modern life delivers full-born (instant, just add water), books represent the life of thought, feeling, and experience as a *process*. Reading is a journey. In the preface, the author introduces herself, as if some civility is in order, and then issues the standard disclaimer for the tenuous covenant that is writing and reading: for the failure of words to do their work perfectly and for the failure of the reader to understand perfectly. All the same, it is better to have journeyed and misunderstood than to have stayed home.

The first few paragraphs of any good book feel like an undertow, but not the kind you swim against. Permission to enter another world is granted, and soon it is difficult to know who is reading and who is being read. When Shawn and I read together, we never hesitate to blurt out some sentence

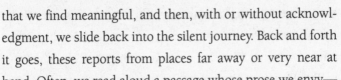

that we find meaningful, and then, with or without acknowl-
edgment, we slide back into the silent journey. Back and forth
it goes, these reports from places far away or very near at
hand. Often, we read aloud a passage whose prose we envy—
something that we know is true but has not been said this
well before: "Listen to this!"

But by far the most important thing that books provide us
is the best means for developing the most vital human faculty:
the *imagination*. Words can describe, but it takes a reader to
conjure up images, to shape them, and, if necessary, to censor them. Our children are committing too many physical
crimes these days because too many *visual* crimes have been
committed against them. Graphic images of violence are being hung in the gallery of their minds without first being
checked at the door. The people who bring us "special effects"
have a moral responsibility not to "burn" such things into
psychic places that were meant to stay green.

Unlike the visual arts, books leave us humanely in charge
of that process by which images move from type to flesh.
Sadly, our society mocks this process with the pejorative
phrase "It's only your imagination." But what else can save us,
if not this silent, essential transportation of the soul? Most human cruelty would be eliminated if people had the capacity
to imagine. As a prerequisite to empathy, imagination makes
kindness possible by allowing us to inhabit the skins we
weren't born in. Lack of imagination, on the other hand,

makes the inflicting of pain, in all its forms, possible. Never are we more honest about cruelty, prejudice, or abuse than when we begin, "You can not *imagine* how it feels. . . ."

Finally, the reading of books is not just a simple, disease-free kind of fantasy. It's an unending means of self-discovery, a means by which the very character of the reader is tutored. In a world where people feel queasy discussing anything more important than the weather, books lure even the most reluctant of us into deep water, into lucid and poetic conversation about things that *really* matter. When gifted writers express what we already know to be true, we recognize our own thoughts and take them more seriously. Raised to their level of conversation, our own discourse becomes more lucid. In short, writers raise the stakes of the game and dare us to contemplate the world as keenly as they do.

Here then is the *third* prescription for the recovery of simple pleasures and the sacramental life: buy, borrow, or check out lots of books, and consider them friends. Some day, when reading to children is as natural as nursing, adults will never be weaned from the page. To be read to before bedtime should be a birthright, so that when we grow up, the itty-bitty-book-light will run down its batteries before the remote control. Parents will take their kids to the library more often than to day care, and teachers will read to students for a sacred hour every day.

People will censor books "aesthetically"—by not buying

them—and kids will be given a book allowance in addition to their regular allowance, so long as they come home with the goods. Books will be bound instead of banned, given as gifts, discussed more often than sports, and elevated by three simple words to the level of a kinder and gentler form of competition: "Have you read . . . ?" Count calories if you like, but go ahead and gorge yourself on books. What have you got to lose but a small mind?

IV

~~~~~~

Parenting:
Big Gods
and Little Gods

> Children begin by loving their parents;
> as they grow older they judge them;
> sometimes they forgive them.
>
> —*Oscar Wilde*

Parenting is the most important job that any human has who chooses (or happens) to reproduce. Unfortunately, no one knows how to do it to begin with, and by the time you figure it out, the kids are grown up and gone—leaving behind the one great guaranteed gift of children to their parents: *guilt.*

So much guilt, in fact, that whole industries exist to deal with it. Books promise to teach parenting, and therapists promise to undo the damage of parenting. Courts get into the act, suggesting that children sue their parents for raising them improperly. One can only assume that the logical consequence is that eventually parents will sue their children for failure to develop properly.

Politicians promise a return to "family values," though never before has a piece of rhetoric been so elastic or so potentially cruel. Rooted in nostalgia rather than reality, this all-purpose phrase leaves out too many people. What's wrong with families is not the result of the wrong party in office, but the acute failure of the most indulged of all generations to view life itself as something other *than* a party. The Woodstock experience may have defined a whole generation, but raising kids is the real trip.

Take that uniquely American social barometer: the beer commercial. Imagine what would happen if aliens landed on this planet and were forced to watch nothing but beer commercials. What would they conclude? Undoubtedly, they would report that life on earth is one long series of predatory nights, where exceptionally tall women wait dewy-eyed in smoky bars for the arrival of a stubble-chinned white knight, his sleeves rolled up for hunting and his European horse being revved up outside by envious valets! Or perhaps the conclusion would be that beer trucks and beer bottles have genie-like properties and can transform the desolate desert truck stop into Friday Night at Fanny Hill's, complete with catered centerfolds.

Compare this to dirty diapers, colic, messy rooms, broken curfews, insolence, rebellion, insubordination, never-ending expenses, and inferior friends, and you begin to grasp the distance between life as advertised and life as lived. Kids literally *steal* your life, draining your energy like little vampires. While beer commercials use the slogan "It doesn't get any better than this!," being a parent operates by a different credo: "It's difficult to *begin* with, and it never *gets* easy."

Part of our problem, of course, is that children are too often regarded as accessories, chips off the old designer block, scrubbed and radiant extras for the backseat of the mini-van. Too infrequently are they seen as little people, searching for order and meaning in the world—even religion—right in their own homes.

One of the best literary metaphors for life is also a wise way to approach the task of raising children. In *Pilgrim's Progress*, Bunyan describes life as a "vale of soul-making." Good things happen and bad things happen. We get some things we want; others are delayed or denied altogether. The point is not to ask: What have you acquired? The real question goes deeper: What effect has all this had on your character? As we pass *from* God *to* God, the most important thing we can ask ourselves is this: How goes it with our soul?

Eastern religion, including Lao-tzu and the Buddha, teaches us that life is not about acquisition and accomplishment, but about the process of *enlightenment*—choosing "the way," or "the eightfold path." Our society often teaches us that nothing of value comes from defeat or disappointment, except as it indicts the ability of the one who failed. Get up, dust yourself off, and try again, we say. Nice guys finish last. Play

vale — Valley

to win, or don't play at all. Winning isn't everything, it's the only thing.

But parenthood teaches a far different lesson. It's not a contest with prizes. It's a process with consequences. Mothers and fathers are gods in the house, the Big gods. Children are gods in training, the Little gods. The house is the temple where life's liturgy is played out, and worship is twenty-four hours a day. When the Big gods are happy, all is well with the Little gods. But when there's trouble above, there's trouble below.

When Shawn and I have an argument and the exchange gets heated, we will often pause to hear, in a distant part of the house, the children arguing. If, on the other hand, we are being affectionate, considerate, and kind to one another, the children will often treat each other likewise—even a brother and sister!

This is frightening—to know that as parents you make or break the faith. But there is no fooling the Little gods, and no amount of *Ozzie and Harriet* incense waved over a temple of constant discord can make the Little gods feel like singing.

This Big god/Little god metaphor is more than theoretical. Once, when Shawn and I returned home from a week-long trip, our two older children greeted us by insisting that we go immediately to the bedroom to see what was waiting there. With luggage still in hand, we huffed straight back to collect our surprise and saw something so remarkable that if it hadn't really happened it would embarrass me to talk about it.

There, on a makeshift altar of satin scraps draped over shoe boxes, were two large photographs of Shawn and me, carefully propped up and nestled into a string of beads and surrounded by several personal artifacts that symbolized the two of us. It was a shrine, not unlike those which adorn the backyards of devout Catholics, especially the poor in Central and South America. In the absence of the Big gods, and in the very room where the Big gods slept, argued, and made love, the Little gods had constructed a token of their devotion. Marking the place as holy, they might just as well have piled up a few stones, poured oil over them, "and called the place Peniel," for to them, "Surely God was in this place."

They were too young at the time to be inhibited about this shameless act of love, but we knew what it meant. The Little gods *watch our every move*; they soak up whatever bliss or vinegar is available in the house. Either it makes them weightless, or it makes them sour. Theologian Horace Bushnell, known for his gentle theories of Christian education, put it perfectly when he said of children: "The odor of the house is always in their garments."

This is not to say that children expect some sort of ethereal bliss to rule the Temple. It's not perfection but commitment they want, first between the Big gods themselves, and then to the idea that the Little gods are worthy, *inherently* worthy. When asked to recount their best times together, grown children hardly ever talk about Disneyland. They remember the day the lights went out and they talked by candlelight until midnight; or they remember the storm they drove through near Pratt, Kansas, when right down to the smallest god they were sure it was the middle of a tornado. They remember rising early to fish with father, or the sight of mother bundled against the cold to watch the soccer game.

You see, the Little gods are never quite sure that the Big gods wouldn't prefer to be absolved of their responsibilities, enjoying their dominion alone. They know that often they are a disappointment and a nuisance. That's why when a Big god sits down and braids the hair of a Little god for an hour, heaven itself opens to reveal that the nature of love is bound up with the inverse use of power. That's why, of all the gifts that a parent can give to a child, *time* is the most precious.

This then is the *fourth* prescription for a more sacramental life full of simple pleasures: if you have children, consider parenthood a high and holy art, until death parts you from their constant gaze. Remember that children crave limits and secretly thrive on a wholesome kind of discipline. They will learn to navigate time, to cherish tenderness, to temper judgment, to remember birthdays, to defend the weak, to notice beauty, to endure inequity, to preserve humility in success and integrity in failure, to care about ideas, to be generous, and to be faithful—all by watching the sermon that is their parents' lives.

Children need chores to do and an allowance to spend. They need compromise on little things and an unwavering resolve on big things. They need an evening set aside just for them, when the Big gods come to visit their world and play in it without making them feel foolish. They need more praise and less ridicule, more patience and less resentment, more love and less shuffling about from one form of abandonment to another.

Ours is not yet a world fit for children. To make it so, we will have to reconstruct the meaning of the "good life." For children, life is good when there's more light in the house than darkness. After all, what the Little gods want is for the Big gods to be happy, and to give them just a little more time.

V

Owning Pets: The Importance of Four-Legged Friends

It is God whom human beings know
in every creature.

—*Hildegard of Bingen*

If it had been left up to me, we wouldn't have gotten the dog. Dogs cost money, they chew up things, they mess all over the house, they get sick and require health care at a time when lots of humans can't afford it. They have to be boarded, dipped, neutered, and fenced. If they bite somebody, you get sued; if they get fleas, the fleas can get in the carpet and then jump on the kids. Then one day, they go out and get hit by a car and break your heart. Is this worth it? It's worth it.

Seven years ago, without explicit permission (but lacking any explicit prohibition) my wife and children brought home a black Labrador retriever puppy and presented it to me as a new member of our family. The adoption, they reasoned, could be refused only by the most hideous of monsters. This was the strategy of their back-door covenant, and when asked whether it was all right to make Maxae a permanent resident, I was forced to answer while staring into her big, brown eyes.

Since that time, I've had no reason to change my mind about the practicality of pets. But I've had plenty of opportunities to witness their emotional, and even spiritual, significance. Animals have a way of bringing out more tenderness from human beings than almost anything else, and they connect us with childhood in a way that isn't childish.

Sociologists have argued that the city is not a natural habitat for human beings. Stacked on top of one another, sealed in by hot concrete, and crammed into cubicles all day long, city dwellers lose contact not only with open space but with the soothing quality of nonhuman life.

As a child, I had the opportunity to make many visits to my grandfather's farm in Henryetta, Oklahoma. It was a small farm with two ponds (in one of which I caught the fish of my dreams), a small herd of cattle, and the usual assortment of chickens, roosters, and pigs.

Looking back on it, I realize that the farm was a magical place for lots of reasons, not the least of which was the presence of animals. They all seemed like pets to me, until my grandmother used an iron bar once to pinch off the head of a chicken for supper, and the decapitated body continued running around the yard for a few minutes, spurting blood. That's when I knew that my worldview was a bit naive.

Just the same, this was the only place where I saw cows close up, with their huge brown eyes and their dumb, wondering stares. It was the only place where I could visit a real barn, fragrant with the sweet smell of alfalfa hay; touch brown and white eggs still warm in a nest; watch milk squirted into a bucket instead of chilled under plastic in the dairy case; and see pigs, with their noses permanently wet and their skin blotched and fuzzy like an old man's chin.

The reason to visit the farm, of course, was to see my grandparents—salt of the earth. But the farm was also where the animals were, and the animals changed me, unaware. For one thing, they connected me to those "lower" branches on the evolutionary tree. Who's to say I wasn't looking at myself, upstream on that gene pool river that ultimately took a primate detour? How much consciousness, I wondered, lay behind those bovine stares? What sort of dreams does a chicken have? Animals stand between us and voiceless matter as a kind of solemn reminder of the scattershot ways of nature. There but for a million mutations go I.

What's more, animals teach us about the elemental forces of life, stripped of artificiality and appearances. They are parables of self-sufficiency, whose only real concern in life is whether an action increases or decreases their chance of survival. They live unburdened by concerns for their reputation—which is precisely their benefit to humans.

It is this very "non-humanness" that tends to make us more humane. Animals ask for nothing but to be taken care of, and (in the case of more conventional pets) to be shown affection. They do not second-guess us, plot against us, get insanely jealous of affection shown to other animals, or nag us constantly about how much happier they might be in a bigger doghouse.

It is the simplicity of animals, and the chance they provide us to show affection without an agenda, that lowers the blood pressure and brings us back down to earth. Around humans, especially in the midst of families, they also provide an escape valve. I have seen my teenage son be affectionate with the dog at times when showing the same affection to me would have been difficult. In fact, it may be that pets provide a kind of safety valve for children, giving them an opportunity to be tender toward something that craves their attention without asking anything in return. As parents are to children, so can children be to pets—providing for them, showing concern for them, and seeing to their well-being in ways that make the children feel like the parents. This is good training for the real thing.

The mystics have written about the importance of what they called "our four-legged friends." They argue that our treatment of animals is a dependable measure, ethically speaking, of our treatment of the very young or the very old. When the apostle Paul wrote that "we who are strong ought to bear the infirmities of the weak," he was making the ulti-mate statement about the relationship between the powerful and the powerless.

That's why all those animal rights activists, however kooky

they seem sometimes, are being essentially faithful to the notion that the strong have an obligation to the weak that goes beyond exploitation. Why *should* we blind rabbits to test our cosmetics? Why *should* we eat red meat when it not only harms us, but requires grazing lands that destroy vital forests? And why should we *not* be concerned about the daily tally of extinctions, except for the fact that the animal strands which break daily are corded together in a rope that holds us above the abyss of our own extinction?

Show me a man who treats well those without status or power—waitresses, taxicab drivers, busboys, bellhops, shoeshiners, the mentally retarded paperboy—and I'll show you a true gentleman who understands that the way the strong relate to the weak is the ultimate ethical test. Keeping animals reminds us of this. It brings out of us a paradoxical strength, a soulful restraint.

Our family dog is now invested with a personal dignity and lifestyle rights that cause the children to chastise their own father (who thinks the dog belongs outside). On a cold night, I hear a self-assured and almost righteous refrain: "Max *must* stay inside the house for heaven's sake . . . do you want her to freeze?" If someone forgets to feed her, it is a crime against simple dignity, a growling, hissing crack in the gentility of the cosmos. If she is injured, she will be bound over to the care of a vet regardless of the cost, just like one of the children.

If it had been left up to me, we wouldn't have gotten the dog. But there is too much practicality in this world and not enough tenderheartedness. Here then is the *fifth* prescription for a life that is both simpler and more sacramental: bring the animals inside—literally or figuratively. Let your actions toward animals be the measure of your compassion toward life itself. Remember Schweitzer's credo: *Reverence for Life.* Keep and cherish your pets. Demonstrate by your care for them how foolish are the ways of love, and how spendthrift are the ways of mercy.

All parents know that one of the first transgressions by very young children is that moment when they decide to rough up a pet—squeeze it until it squeaks, or box its ears because, after all, it can't tattle on them. This is a crucial moment for stopping cruelty in its tracks. It gives parents their first chance to talk about the ethics of power and powerlessness: never hurt an animal, needlessly.

Once, when one of our guinea pigs died prematurely, my daughter, Chelsea, prepared a grave for it in the garden. She borrowed a small piece of marble that her mother uses for art and etched the letters P-I-G near the top. Once this simple headstone was in place, she held some sort of brief ceremony and then laid the pig to rest in the shade of the tomato plants. A few days later, a wild pink poppy flowered in just that spot, a happening that Shawn ascribed to the fertility of Pig's spirit. Now, every spring, we all dig carefully around the grave, so as not to disturb Pig's resting place or the fond memories of her time in the house.

What was Chelsea doing? She was "bearing the infirmities of the weak." She was making a practice run at grief, just as every goodbye is a practice run at death. She was making noble that which the world has no reason to remember, and giving a name to the nameless lost. If this isn't simple and sacramental, nothing is.

VI

Letters and Gifts:
The Considerate Life

I am in the habit of looking not so much
to the nature of the gift as to the spirit
in which it is offered.

—*Robert Louis Stevenson*

Never before in human history has so much dazzling technology made it possible to communicate so quickly and so clearly with so many—across the street or across the continents. And yet despite all this, we are starved for messages that mean something. We talk in our cars, ordering food through a speaker ("Would you like fries or a cherry pie with that?"), and we fax our promises through phone lines. But we have forgotten the art of writing letters; we have lost the basic vocabulary of concern; we are all business and no heart, all fast food—and no soul food.

From the stranger on the other end of the telephone at dinnertime who pretends to be a friend, concerned for our well-being ("Mr. Meyers, how are you doing this evening?") to the junk mail disguised as checks or audits or letters from a law firm, Americans are besieged by insincerity. We choke on feigned familiarity. Electronic begging erodes courtesy and turns us into cynics who dread to pick up the phone at meal-time.

It all serves to explain the actions of an old woman I knew once who used to drag a lawn chair out into her yard every time she went for the mail. One day, watching her, I asked what the chair was for. She looked at me and smiled and said, "I'm trying to get up high enough to reach way in the back of the box. That's where the little ones are, the handwritten ones, the cards and notes."

Her reach to the back of the box symbolizes a whole society that is yearning for thoughtful, honest, and affectionate communication. None of us is an "occupant" or "current resident." We have names, and we want to see them written or typed on the front of the envelope, not bar-coded or computer-generated. We want to hear from some*one* who knows us and cares enough to send us a word.

Once upon a time, letters were the standard vehicle of courtship. They were thoughtful, contemplative, and considerate. They were the imprint of our dreams, swirling under cursive dress. They were the artifacts of emotion—intimacy expressing itself as art. Considerably beyond mere communication, letters, especially love letters, are addressed to the *soul*.

Thomas Moore, in *Soul Mates*, has reminded us that envelopes are one of the few things in the modern world that we seal, thus creating a private space for expression. And stamps are not merely tokens of monetary exchange, but small paintings, the closest thing we have to medieval miniature art.

In letters we tend to choose our words carefully and to imagine the reader's response. To leave in, or to leave out, to create this impression or that one—these are the considerations of art, and art is the channel to the soul. Letters also carry a sense of importance and cannot be interrupted, as speech can, before the entire experience is complete. Composed, they also compose us.

Like books, letters are tangible things, more reflective than coercive. They "disembody" the voice and hence capture a good deal more of the soul than ordinary discourse, which is too often designed to win, rather than to communicate. Saving a stack of old letters is likewise a tradition that elevates the art of letter writing and the joy of receiving them. We owe the existence of most of the New Testament to this custom.

For the simple and sacramental life, thoughtful and artful self-expressions are the hallmarks of intimacy and the couriers of contentment. If the long-lost art of letter writing were to be retrieved, the world would be much better for it. And there is yet another simple practice which, if not lost, has been largely stylized: the giving of gifts.

Our society has preserved this custom but compromised it by both obligation and excess. Birthdays, anniversaries, graduations, baby showers, bridal dowries—all carry with them the *expectation* of gift-giving. And this is not all bad when we consider that very few young couples could start a household without wedding gifts. Shawn and I still look at a glass bowl given to us by one of my father's parishioners, and we remember with gratitude the practicality of social obligations.

Unfortunately, wedding invitations sent to us now suggest a willingness to accept "cash in lieu of gifts," and we realize that the spirit of gift-giving is often replaced by the crassest form of greed. Add to this the Christmas morning frenzy, where the children have barely opened one present before they abandon it to rip gleefully into the next, and a feeling begins to descend upon us that gift-giving has become just another compulsion.

What we might consider more often is the *occasionless* gift, the token of simple affection and consideration. Take a bottle of wine along when someone else has cooked your dinner; pick some wildflowers and arrange them in a vase upon your arrival; purchase the book a friend has wanted to read; share the excess of your summer garden; bring along a clipping, a cartoon, an editorial that made you think of someone or made you laugh. But most of all, consider a gift of something you have created yourself.

Many people forget that this does not require artistic talent. A woman in my church bakes the finest pies in the known universe. She enjoys bringing them to me as much as I enjoy eating them. I brag about her pies incessantly; she bakes them religiously (I use the word advisedly), and to-gether we form one of the most pleasant and dependable of human dyads: the gift *giver* and the gift *receiver*.

People forget sometimes that every gift needs a willing and unapologetic recipient. I never say to Mrs. Bell, "Oh, you shouldn't have" or "How can I repay you" or "No thanks, I'm on a diet." I say, "God bless you, put them down right over there . . . care for a piece?" We all have something to give one another, and it's not a competition. It's a form of commu-nion.

Between husbands and wives, lovers and friends, a thoughtful gift may be one of the most gracious and renew-ing of human acts. Men will often buy lingerie (the gift that keeps on giving), but it would be wise to consider something disconnected from one's own pleasure, facilitating instead someone else's. For example, a plane ticket to go alone and visit a friend; a new set of paintbrushes for the artist; a gift certificate good for so many hours of babysitting.

Sometimes the oft-heard phrase "It's the thought that counts" is little more than a form of apology. What people re-ally crave is not the object per se, but a gift which in itself in-dicates *thoughtfulness*. It serves to remind us, as Marsilio Fi-cino writes, that friends are those "who live in each other's hearts."

On a recent trip to San Francisco to perform a christening, I went looking for gifts for my own children. In the past, I have done it poorly, even succumbing at times to that over-priced bastion of absentee-father-guilt: the airport gift shop. But this time, I pledged to do it better, even if that meant doing it differently. Chelsea is a swimmer and wished most of all to be brought a new swimming suit—especially if it was flattering and locally unavailable, thus giving her an exotic advantage in explaining it to friends.

Blue, along with a zillion other adolescents, wears Mossimo shirts. This bothers me, and he knows it, because I too often make comments about the lemming-like conventions of fashion. So, instead of a rare book or a shark's tooth, I decided that day to buy him what he actually wanted—a rather strange-looking shirt with the coveted brand name. And for Chelsea, a black one-piece suit with a Harley-David-son-like symbol on the front that read "Born to Swim."

Blue put his shirt on immediately and wore it for a week, until we persuaded him that washing it was also a good idea. Chelsea wore the suit to swim practice every day and never seemed to tire of my telling her how flattering it looked on her. They both thanked me more times than was necessary, and I have had ample opportunity to reflect upon what all this means. Whether we always know what to get, or even how to receive what is given, it is surpassingly important to know that we live in one another's hearts—what's more, that such habitation is so important that it alters the paths we walk and changes the shape of our day.

This, then, is the *sixth* prescription, in two parts, for the sacramental life of simple pleasures: put your hand to paper again, and script the shape of your heart by writing a letter. There need be no special occasion, just the desire to express yourself and to mail a piece of your soul. And when you can, imagine what sort of gift will make someone smile, and then give it for no other reason. To know that we "inhabit someone's heart" is to live.

VII

Seizing
the Moment

I think we would be able to live in this world
more peaceably if our spirituality
were to come from looking not just
into infinity but very closely at the
world around us—and appreciating
its depth and divinity.

— Thomas Moore

If there is one constant message that all the saints have tried to communicate through the centuries it is this: live the moment. Consider the possibility that in every waking hour, a sacred theater is in session, played out before an audience that is largely blind. Until this blindness is overcome, there is no revelation. What we need is to acquire what Ricoeur called a "second naiveté."

We have all become dull of spirit because we think the world is ordinary. Seventeenth-century Dutch painter Johannes Vermeer is said to have made masterpieces out of nothing—a woman reading a letter or asleep at a table. Critics call his work the "timeless contemplation of the ordinary" and "eternalizing the moment." That should be everyone's pastime, because "luminescence," as Annie Dillard puts it, can break through the most mundane of moments—but only if we recover the eyes of childhood. As another woman put it: "I am still foolishly amazed that my morning coffee actually *stays* in the cup, and steam dances above it, and rises into my nose like the gift of waking."

Although it sounds like the stuff of a freshman philosophy class, the most important question we can ask is simply this: Why is there *anything*? What caused the universe to *be* in the first place, and what sort of Mind drives this delicate, terrifying mess? Shaken loose of late from our former assumptions about a mechanistic, Newtonian world of order and predictability, we experience the world now as a far stranger and less predictable place than we ever imagined. Watching the "experts" predict the path of a hurricane is a good example of this.

Even though the name is paradoxical, one of the lessons of chaos theory is that an unfathomable order exists, a magnificent interconnectedness from one end of the cosmos to the other—we just can't see it from our finite perspective. We look "at" things instead of "through" them. As Archibald MacLeish lamented: "We await the rebirth of wonder."

It is not this way with children. They are born wide-eyed and wonderful. And if we watch them closely, they can teach us things that we have forgotten. My first son, Blue, taught me that if we watch the world closely, we can see wonderful things. Once, when he was two, he gave me an unforgettable moment of innocence and wisdom.

I was a doctoral student at the Theological School of Drew University in Madison, New Jersey, and a student pastor in Summit. My toddler son liked to pull me away from my typewriter and into his world as often as possible. It was Advent season, and I was working on a sermon. Blue had other ideas. This is how I recorded it in an essay for the Oakes Memorial church newsletter under the title "No Wolf, No Wolf!"

Advent is a time when we celebrate small things which later emerge as significant out of all proportion to their size. In our faithful imaginings, a sleeping infant will be called King. Lowly shepherds will get the word ahead of *The New York Times*, and instead of rushing to the wire, they will return to tending their sheep, as if to think on it awhile, as if satisfied that the secret was intended for the likes of them.

In a damp and crooked barn somewhere under a proud star, time itself will be reordered. God will take a stand, and the only sword will be a baby's rhythmic breathing. As a witness to the truth of these fantasies, the Church will keep on straining with hope to feel the wonder of little things . . . and worshipers will escape the burden of a Big God for a moment and peer through a key-hole at the Mystery.

As if this were not enough, my family welcomes little boy Blue to his second wide-eyed Christmas. Besides another joyous thing, he is a fascinating package of promise. Seeds are planted every day in him that may be dormant for years, while others, some good, some bad, seem to germinate overnight. Just the other day, one of these "plantings" took place, and I can't help but wonder when, if ever, it will blossom.

It is a sunlit November morning, and Shawn has gone off to school. Blue requests his morning favorite: Bunny Stories. How and why these storytelling sessions have come to be called Bunny Stories is hard to tell, but it really doesn't matter. Blue uses their magic power to rescue me from my office, which he must think bores me as much as it bores him. Up goes that velvet little hand, "cheesy" goes the grin, and off goes captive Daddy.

To the sitting room, where white late autumn sun splashes bars across the parsonage floor. There we pile on the couch, Blue squats cross-legged on my chest, and the unrehearsed tales begin. It doesn't matter what exploits the Bunny may encounter, so long as there are a few "big trucks" in the story. And it doesn't matter how

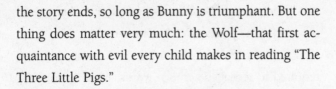

the story ends, so long as Bunny is triumphant. But one thing does matter very much: the Wolf—that first acquaintance with evil every child makes in reading "The Three Little Pigs."

What I discover that morning is that Blue is strenuously opposed to the appearance of the Wolf in any other story—especially as a threat to his beloved Bunny. This becomes obvious when I decide to liven up an otherwise floundering Bunny Story with a little Wolf attack. "Out of the woods he comes, the wicked old wolf, and grabs the Bunny!"

"No Wolf! No Wolf!" shouts Blue, his face etched with a concern too deep for skin like his. The brows drop, the eyes grow bright, and he reaches out to cover my mouth with his tiny hand. As long as I am silent, the Bunny is safe, and not even my earnest apology can stop his anguished protest: "No Wolf ! No Wolf!"

I try some crude foreshadowing: "The Bunny will win, Blue, believe me. The Bunny will escape without a scratch." That doesn't work. I even offer to send the monster back into the woods without a confrontation, explaining that Bunny just wasn't his cup of tea. This doesn't work either. Finally, I say we will just leave the stupid wolf in the woods where he belongs. Even this isn't good enough. Blue wants him *out of the story*. And only when he is completely satisfied that there is no wolf at all can the story continue. This means that I am required to repeat the crucial words, which I do: "OK, son . . . no wolf, no wolf."

This harmless little moment charmed me at first, but the more I thought about it, the more significant and meaningful it seemed. Days passed and Blue all but forgot his urgent protest, but I didn't. It dawned on me that something marvelous had flashed across the screen of his mind, and I had been there to see it. A picture of innocence so pure that he could not have been aware of how transparently beautiful it was.

You see, it wasn't just a case of "ignorance is bliss," because even at age two, Blue had been introduced to evil, or he wouldn't have feared the wolf at all. But his soul was as yet unclouded by a single malicious thought. So he thought nothing of editing the world to make it conform to his own. In his world, free from harm, there was no need to look over your shoulder. The sound of footsteps meant the approach of a friend; he was on good terms with the night; and violence had never proved itself a useful thing. It couldn't rock like Mommy, hug like Daddy, or comfort like a bottle of milk—so who needed it?

And all the while I thought of Calvin, who would tell me

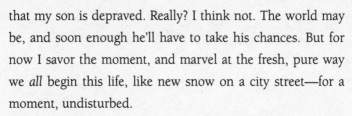

that my son is depraved. Really? I think not. The world may be, and soon enough he'll have to take his chances. But for now I savor the moment, and marvel at the fresh, pure way we *all* begin this life, like new snow on a city street—for a moment, undisturbed.

Because it won't be long now until his friends come knocking, fresh from watching a violent movie—with comics to trade, and stories to tell, and every other word will be "Zap," "Pow," or "Bang." "Can Blue go with us to see Godzilla—he eats all the people in New York City!" And what does my son say? *Cool?* What about the Bunny?

Forget it, Dad, and get back to work on your sermon. Don't just practice what you preach, *believe it*. Make this the *seventh* prescription for the life of simple pleasures and sacramental living: seize the day, but don't hold it by the throat. Trust the rain to break the drought, and trust the power of life's unfolding. Someday, Blue may have a child sitting crosslegged on his chest, a child that needs reassurance. Then he can complete the circle, and can say, in his own words, in his own time, out of his own primal memory: "No Wolf . . . No Wolf."

VIII

Romancing the Home

Sex and beauty are inseparable, like life
and consciousness. And the intelligence
which goes with sex and beauty, and
arises out of sex and beauty, is intuition.

—*D. H. Lawrence*

Our society, much like the fabled Roman civilization, is un-
raveling. The reasons are many, but the single greatest force at
work to break the bindings which make us human and preserve the soul is sexual dysfunction. Despite a steady drum-
beat of Puritan criticism, we consume more pornography and
indulge in more narcissistic erotic behavior than any culture
on the face of the earth. We hate sex, we love sex. We are
afraid of it, we are de   ately attracted to it. We claim to be
shocked by what other people are doing, but we pay them to
tell us about it. We campaign against depravity to prove our
decency, and then we descend into the pit of sexual compulsion at the risk of losing everything we say is important to us:
marriage, career, family, basic human trust.

Sex. It compels us and it makes us queasy. We can't decide

whether it's some sort of unfortunate biological lag, pulling us in the direction of animals, or a sacred delirium to be joined with the spirit in ways that make us fully human. As the world's oldest commodity, it is also the world's most effectively mass-produced cause of anxiety and paranoia. About nothing else on earth is the grass always so much greener on the other side of the fence. We live for illusions at the expense of possibilities.

These days, it seems that much of American politics is driven by differing views of human sexuality. Most of the so-called hot-button issues are sexual in nature. The way to win elections now is not to get people to vote *for* you, but to persuade them to vote *against* a morally inferior opponent. It's called the "politics of allegation," and its bread-and-butter is sexual gossip.

What's more, sexual insecurity, which has been fueling persecution in America since the Salem witch trials, has turned its attention to a new list of enemies. Homophobia can be driven by secret fears that the anxious one himself may be gay; much anti-abortion fervor is driven by an unarticulated desire to make women suffer for their "promiscuity"; and the fear of sex education in the schools is grounded in the notion that honest information about sexuality is an incentive to sexual misconduct. The truth is, nothing encourages destructive sexual behavior so much as righteous denial, ritual secrecy, and institutional fear. The apostle Paul has it right when he says that he might not have lusted so much had someone not said in a such a loud voice: "Thou shalt not lust!"

If there is any hope at all of curing what ails us sexually, it will be grounded in a healthier, more natural view of this powerful human instinct. If families are going to be stitched back together again, it will have to begin with confession: nowhere do we sow the seeds of a healthy or unhealthy sexuality with more "fertility" than at home. Nowhere do we teach the wrong lessons more powerfully than when the Big gods fail to show the Little gods that physical attraction and affection are divine attributes, mysterious and dangerous, too important to ignore, too wonderful to deny, too sublime to keep hidden away.

The home is the Temple of Eros. It is there that children first experience physical attraction and affection as either sacred or profane. When the Little gods see the Big gods embrace, love itself gets bolted down to the soul. When parents hold hands, children see tenderness in action. When there is an embrace in the kitchen, then the private passion of the bedroom is validated, rather than divorced from real life. Mothers and fathers who kiss in front of their children may hear "Yuk!," but what they hear if they listen more closely is "Ahhh."

What's more, when the Big gods live out their respect for sexual boundaries, they establish those same boundaries in their children. When they are affectionate within the covenant of marriage, they pass along the sexual importance of covenant to their children. There are lots of different opinions out there on what constitutes "the holy," but I am more and more attracted to the notion that the truly sacred is found in that "space between." This is the lesson of Martin Buber's *I/Thou*: that whether between nations and God, or between partners in committed relationships, the real "holy of holies" is that world created by the intersection of two people in love with more than themselves—people whose love and trust find *reciprocity*. The Quakers like to think of God as a divine spark within each soul. Perhaps it is really a spark *between* two souls.

Whether Freud was right about the Oedipus complex or not, any parent knows that when an infant crawls into the parental bed, he will crawl into that spot between his mother and father. In what constitutes an almost instinctive form of communion, he puts himself between them, as if to be charged by the energy which must now pass *through* him. My infant son will often turn and push me away—not so much to "replace me," as Freud might say, as to practice *being* me.

That's why it is so important that the simple and sacramental life be a life of *demonstrated* affection. A religious view of life is by nature a sensuous one—not to consume for the sake of pleasure, but to embrace for the sake of delight. To compliment and to caress are the true signs of romance, and they teach by example a life of *consideration*. Show me a home where there is no physical intimacy, and I'll show you a home where affection is really an "affectation."

But show me a home where the Big gods hold hands, hold faces, and hold hearts, and I'll show you little romantics in training—children who will find it harder to separate love and sex when it's their turn to run the Temple. The theory once was: never fight in front of your children, and never kiss in front of them either. The result? A whole generation which assumed that passion in all its forms was a thing to be feared and hidden and that romance always precedes marriage but never sustains it.

This then is the *eighth* prescription for the recovery of a simpler and more sacramental life: make holy the space *between* you by showing simple affection. Let your children see you kiss. Let them see you embrace. Let them overhear your teasing, your gentle rebukes, even your well-intentioned jealousy. Domestic courtship reinforces the notion that people are together because they *want* to be together, not because it's the decent, practical thing to do.

Perhaps that's the trouble with trying to turn the best things in life into some sort of investment strategy, where everything is weighed and measured. Actions are considered worthwhile if they "get us something." Romance is merely a prelude to seduction, and simple acts of kindness (like fresh flowers) are used to cover our mistakes, or make our apologies. Genuine romance, on the other hand, is sufficient unto itself and need not be part of some larger, self-serving strategy.

The fact is, all impractical gestures of affection are grounded in the belief that no one ever outgrows the need to be surprised by signs of their worth in the eyes of others. And these signs need not be lavish. Cut some flowers out of a garden, even a vacant lot, and arrange them on the dinner table; take an interest in what colors are pleasing to the one you love, and remember them when buying a gift; take time to listen; telephone for no reason but to say that you were thinking about the other person and that he or she matters; compliment some physical feature that attracts you, even if you've done it many times before; buy something you know the other will like, regardless of whether *you* like it; take over the chores that are not normally yours, and give the gift of a few hours of peace and quiet.

When you have a little extra money, don't always do the most practical thing you can, like buying tires for the car. Once in a while, a man should take a woman shopping for a dress—and then make sure she has an occasion to wear it. Every married couple should schedule times away from family, work, and the pressures of social life to rediscover what attracted them to each other in the first place. Don't worry about the children. They are the ones who will benefit most from having parents who are lovers.

And remember: do not give up *dancing*, just because you

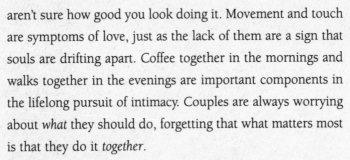

aren't sure how good you look doing it. Movement and touch are symptoms of love, just as the lack of them are a sign that souls are drifting apart. Coffee together in the mornings and walks together in the evenings are important components in the lifelong pursuit of intimacy. Couples are always worrying about *what* they should do, forgetting that what matters most is that they do it *together*.

Relationships are a *pilgrimage*, and they unfold with an equal measure of challenge and possibility. But they cannot survive the loss of intimacy or the loss of consideration. When you think about it, saving the last dance for someone you love isn't just a quaint remnant of an old-fashioned hospitality. It may be the best hope you have of dancing again.

IX

The Religion
of Mercy

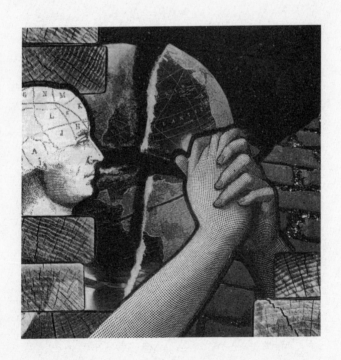

For I desired mercy, and not sacrifice;
and the knowledge of God more
than burnt offerings.

— *Hosea*

On a bright spring morning, three days after Easter in Oklahoma City, a clean-cut but lonesome drifter with a pathological hatred for the U.S. government drove a truck packed with homemade explosives to the front door of the Alfred P. Murrah Federal Building and blew a gaping hole in the myth of the American Heartland.

Bottle-fed on Hate Radio, and estranged from everything and everyone, including himself, this crusader against the Evil One has finally shown us what the politics of fear can produce: sow enough bad seeds, and eventually you harvest a mutant crop.

This is the city where I live and work, teach and preach. On the morning of April 19, at two minutes after nine, I am standing in front of a group of sleepy-eyed public-speaking students at Oklahoma City University, taking roll. Without a cloud in the sky, we hear it thunder, and within the hour I stand a few blocks from the most grotesque sight I have ever seen. People wander the streets in shock, and the air is full of the smell of death and the numbness of disbelief. It feels like the first time I got the wind knocked out of me as a child and couldn't get enough of the right kind of air. I ask myself: are we losing our minds, or just our souls?

As an ordained minister, I feel the insult of insults: to be reminded that the "militias" which breed the Timothy McVeighs of this world do so with a Bible in one hand and a gun in the other. The word *Christian* is now being attached to the most violent, the most paranoid, the most dangerous elements of society. Clinic workers are murdered by people calling themselves "pro-life." Under the banner of Jesus, Prince of Peace, we hear more hate-filled rhetoric, see more homophobia, and witness more suspicion of women than from any other group. Christianity has been *hijacked*, and the ugly joyride is far from over.

For all of us who preach the gospel, these are painful times, reminiscent of the refrain of a once popular tune: "Look what they've done to my song." Because the best things in the world are the easiest to corrupt, religion is in constant danger of destroying itself. Millions of intelligent people have already given it up, and yet go on searching for enlightenment and spirituality, often in solitude, disconnected from community.

The religious impulse is universal. In the famous words of Augustine, our hearts really *are* restless, "until they find rest in Thee." In every great religious tradition, the object is to overcome *separation*—from God and from one another. The marks of the truly religious person are the same no matter what name is used for God, and regardless of the rituals employed to "bring down the divine." The person of true faith gets *reconnected*, and the signs of this reunion are unmistakable. No longer a captive to fear and hatred, this mended heart now sees life's chief business as reconciliation, made possible by the only thing that can save us—unconditional love.

The problem comes when revelation gets itself organized into systems, and the systems harden into doctrine. Insight begets teaching begets rules. Before you know it, revelation meant to connect us becomes ecclesiastical doctrine certain to divide us.

There is no better example than Jesus of Nazareth. Just reminding people that he wasn't a Christian will bring bewildered stares from the man on the street. Preacher and theologian Ernest Campbell has summarized the ministry of Jesus thus: a reforming Jew, convinced that his people had turned love into legalism, he went about asking those people who thought they were "in" (Pharisees, Sadducees, and other officially religious people), "Are you sure you're in? . . . I know you *think* you're in, but are you *sure* you're in?" And to those who thought they were "out" (widows, tax collectors, prostitutes, the sick and dispossessed, and other officially irreligious people), he asked, "Are you sure you're out? . . . I know you *think* you're out, but are you *sure* you're out?"

His ministry was one of constant and unbridled compassion, and his parables made the point again and again: our thoughts are not God's thoughts, even on our best days. When the prophets called Israel to examine her faithfulness, the questions were never theological—they were always *ethical*: "How goes it in the land with the stranger, the widow, the orphan?" When Jesus gave his first sermon in his hometown, it was an announcement that he was the fulfillment of Isaiah's prophecy, that God had what Roman Catholic theologians, especially in the Third World, call "a preferential option for the poor." Marcus Borg calls it the "politics of compassion," as opposed to the "politics of purity." But whatever you call it, it certainly wasn't "Jesus, meek and mild, gentle as a little child." After the benediction, they tried to kill him.

So what does all this mean to us, to you and to me—trying to live a simpler and more sacramental life? It means that we will have to examine our religious beliefs to see whether they make us more or less merciful, for any religion that doesn't make us kinder isn't worth our time, and may even be hazardous to our health. Any religion that closes us down instead of opening us up; makes us less tolerant, not more tolerant; builds walls of separation instead of bridges of under-standing must be condemned.

Civilization, from a heavenly point of view, is nothing but the long slow process of learning to be kind. Therefore every religious institution that promises its followers exclusive rights to the kingdom, woos them with the intoxicating drug of certainty, and makes them believe that salvation is reserved for the chosen few must be rejected as the seeds of Holy War, of Inquisition, and of every dark and bloody chapter in the history of organized religion.

This then is the *ninth* prescription for those who wish to live a simpler and more sacramental life: measure your faith by measuring its *mercy*. Ask yourself whether it makes you more likely to forgive and to reconcile, to be patient and self-sacrificing, to put your own house in order before trying to rearrange the rest of the world's furniture.

The sacramental life is a life infused with religious mean-ing, but not the kind that leads to new forms of idolatry. The truly religious person sees nature, life, and mind as a unified whole and is neither compulsive nor controlling. Vanity gives way to gratitude, and every single act, no matter how in-significant, is viewed as meaningful within the mysterious web of life.

What's more, all the conventional definitions of power and prestige are turned on their heads. To be weak in the eyes of the world is to be strong in the eyes of God. To give to the beggar, to strengthen the disinherited, to bring hope to the destitute, and to build up with love and affection what the world is always trying to tear down with cleverness and deceit—this is the measure of the sacramental life.

Do not live to be watched and rewarded. Age gracefully and surrender the ego of youth along with its presumption of immortality. Do not look past the moment in search of some miracle—miracles are *in* the moment. Do not make cheap sport of blaming the poor for being poor, but do what you can to change their lot, and share more of what you have received.

If you happen to be Christian or Jewish, give some thought to what an upside-down world it would be if Mary's song, the Magnificat, were the order of the day. Remember that a penniless rabbi who never wrote anything down changed the world by rendering every square inch of it sacred and by pronouncing every man, woman, and child a beloved son or daughter of God. When it starts to feel too pleasant to be a Christian, too easy, remember that it used to be dangerous—that its Founder was put to death as a common criminal, a victim of capital punishment.

Religion has done more harm and more good in this world than anything else. It should never be trifled with, or worn as a badge of decency. It should never be manipulated for sentimental value or invoked for the sake of advantage—in war or in politics. Its purpose is to reunite a broken world with the Source of every good and perfect gift, to turn feverish little clods of petty grievance and self-absorption into partners in pursuit of the Holy.

The simple life of simple pleasures *is* the religious life, if simple means contented, gracious, and austere. In a world where millions starve in the shadow of bigger and bigger castles, there can be no integrity in a faith that encourages, even blesses, conspicuous consumption. An Oriental visitor to the United States was asked recently what one impression of America stood out above all the rest. She said, almost apologetically: "In my country, we only take what we *need*."

What a novel concept.

~~~~~

Only the Bound
Are Free

> If a nation values anything more than freedom,
> it will lose its freedom; and the irony
> of it is that if it is comfort or money
> that it values more, it will lose that too.

> —*Somerset Maugham*

Every Fourth of July, Americans celebrate the Number One Word in our vocabulary: *freedom*. We spread the word on everything, like jam on bread. We get misty-eyed singing about it, puffed up like peacocks talking about it, and better-dead-than-Red serious about defending it. We love the word so much that we are almost indignant when someone asks us to explain exactly what it means. Some words are like elevator music: we enjoy the nondescript way they soothe us on the way to wherever it is we are going. But if asked to name that tune, we haven't a clue.

Most people would say, without even flinching, that ours is the most free society on earth—and on one level at least, it's true. We have created a society in which people can rise higher and fall farther than anywhere else on earth. We have created more material abundance, and in its shadow more emotional distress, than any other nation can claim. And while hating taxes is still the most popular of political sports, our taxes remain the lowest in the industrialized world. The poor can't pay, and the rich find ways not to, and hence only in America does the middle class (that leaven in the loaf of democracy) provide welfare for *both* the rich and the poor.

As for the idea of freedom, it is mostly a behavioral concept now, rather than a philosophic one. Although cloaked in righteous rhetoric, the word is used mostly to protest the watchful eye of any collective conscience. In other words, freedom means being left alone to do as we please in the pursuit of getting, and keeping, what we want. Freedom, for many, is another word for *secrecy* about the vast inequalities in American life.

Samuel Johnson had this in mind when he uttered those famous words "Patriotism is the last refuge of a scoundrel." It is currently very popular to talk hysterically about how we are all "losing our freedom." But for many, this means anything that crimps their style, adds a detour to the shortest distance between what they have and what they want, and forces them to observe basic humanitarian rules which they insist everyone would observe anyway if just left alone. Is it Adam Smith's "Invisible Hand," or is it really the Little Red Hen Theory of freedom: "I planted the wheat . . . I ground the flour

. . . I baked the cake . . . [and] I'm going to eat it all by myself!"

Yet another, and perhaps more harmful, fiction about human freedom is that it constitutes a pretext for various kinds of *indulgence*—oblivious to its impact on others. Freedom means license to suspend obligation, to consume thoughtlessly, or to seek pleasure irresponsibly. Thus, it is a measure of "freedom" to allow motorcyclists to ride without helmets. But explain that freedom to the widow whose husband's skull is crushed, to her now fatherless children, and to the emergency room crew who labored all night trying to repair what could have been avoided (doctors call them "donor-cycles").

As a young man, I thought freedom had something to do with taking a cross-country motorcycle trip à la *Easy Rider*—the wind in my hair, no schedule, no obligations, nothing but the open road. Now I know the truth: the road has potholes, the wind is full of bugs, and nobody outside of your immediate family cares much whether you live or die.

That's why the simple and sacramental life demands that we recover a *religious* concept of freedom—one that is vastly different from the popular and political one. Religious freedom was once defined as the voluntary embrace of deeper and more sacred obligations than any civil authorities could ever demand. This is the meaning of "rendering unto Caesar that which is Caesar's, and unto God that which is God's." In the New Testament, *only the bound are free*—those who have given up freedom as an excuse for indulgence and are using it instead as a means of surrendering their lives to a higher purpose.

As a UCC minister whose background is Congregational, I know all about the love of freedom, and our near-idolatrous infatuation with Yankee independence as a form of church governance. But "doing what we please" can also mean "doing nothing," and "charity begins at home" can also mean that it *ends* there as well. A wise old preacher said once: "Freedom doesn't mean doing as we please; it means doing what pleases Christ."

This then is the *tenth* prescription for a simpler and more sacramental life: use your freedom to choose what you will *give up* on behalf of others. Don't confuse lack of restraint with a license to move away from obligations, but consider it an opportunity to move toward them. Freedom is about opportunity, not license. Otherwise, it's just another word for selfishness.

It has been said that life is nothing but a series of choices and that, over time, we become what our choices have made us. If we make selfish choices, again and again, we may end up unfettered, but also alone. But if we choose to be in covenant with those around us, we reap far more than we have unselfishly sown. The precious and intoxicating thing about freedom is that it suspends us over life's never-ending decisions: every single day is a fork in the road, an option on tomorrow.

As science moves toward a unified theory of creation, theologians will be asked to join physicists in a reaffirmation of the consequential nature of more than just matter (for every action there is an opposite and equal reaction). We will all soon recognize that in the world of the spirit there is consequentialness as well. For we are saved or damned *because* of what we do more than in *spite* of what we do.

The simple and sacramental life is a *choice*. It is a deliberate act of self-effacement, requiring an option on the road less traveled over the treadmill of self-fulfillment. It begins every morning when the eyes first blink open: Turn the covers over, or go back to sleep? Pet the dog, or growl at it? Start the day with a kind word, or start complaining?

As the day goes on, the stakes grow higher, but the choices never end. Is my work a vocation, or a means to an end? Are my co-workers pawns in a game, or real human beings whose feelings matter? Shall I flirt with the secretary, or call my wife to see how the day is going? Go to the office party, or go to a child's recital? Have a beer with the boys, or make it to the school play on time? Remember birthdays, anniversaries, and dates that matter to someone other than myself, or make a joke about how forgetful I am?

If the Great Evil IRS were not breathing down your neck, would you do your taxes honestly, or would "freedom" mean you could get away with cheating? Without a post office box or a secure phone line, would you be able to carry on the affair? The line between privacy and secrecy is very thin. Full disclosure sounds like a *legal* matter, but it's really a *moral* one. When decisions are made that never see the light of day, the consequences are often the darkest of human behaviors.

How do we make decisions that reflect a simple life and the desire for a more sacramental existence? We pay attention to those people that nobody pays attention to, rather than working our world like a cocktail party. We read to a child, either ours or someone else's. We don't push people aside when they get in our way, as if people constituted hazards on the way to a perfect golf score.

Father Alfred D'Souza said once: "For a long time it had seemed to me that life was about to begin—real life. But there was always some obstacle in the way, something to be got through first, some unfinished business, time still to be served, a debt to be paid. Then life would begin. At last it dawned on me that these obstacles *were* my life."

Should you pick up the phone and call an aging parent, or worry about your phone bill? Should you listen patiently to people when they tell their story, or excuse yourself by saying you're late for a very important date? Should you give to a panhandler, or excuse yourself with reassurances that he will probably spend the money on booze? Should you buy your own stamps, or run your personal mail through the office

postage meter? I'm afraid a whole generation has been confused ever since Janis Joplin belted out: "Freedom's just another word for nothin' left to lose."

Simple pleasures are those moments when life is experi-
enced rather than consumed, and moments are sacramental
when the transcendent infuses the ordinary. But it doesn't ar-
rive like a catered meal driven to the door, and you can't get
there from here even if you hire a limousine. You can't wres-
tle the Good Life to the ground, break its arm, and then de-
clare yourself the winner. It's the backside of a divine bargain,
a trump card that is never played face up. The best things in
the world are freely *given* to those who have freely *chosen* well.

XI

Cook Something, Build Something

As I grew up, Thanksgiving evolved perfectly. It used to be that men had the hard work, which is to sit in the living room and make conversation about gas mileage and lower back pain, and women got the good job, which is cooking. Women owned the franchise, and men milled around the trough mooing, and if any man dared enter the kitchen, he was watched closely lest he touch something and damage it permanently.

— *Garrison Keillor*

It should come as no surprise that at the center of the life and faith of the Church there sits a *table*—likewise that its highest sacrament is a meal, where what is common is consecrated, and what is simple and sparse is pronounced bountiful. Whatever one's theology of communion, the symbolism is consistent with the way in which the teacher revealed the kingdom to his students: do not stare off into space, imagining some far-off place where never is heard a discouraging word, and the skies are not cloudy all day.

One of America's finest teachers of preaching, Fred Craddock, said it best: "I don't think that on the night of the Last Supper, Jesus was heavy into sacramental theology. Maybe he just said, 'Uh, pass me the butt-end of that piece of bread (and they passed it) . . . Any wine left in the goblet? (Yes) . . . Pass it here.' And he took it, and broke it, and blessed it . . . and a supper became a sacrament because he *said so.*"

Today, we have all sorts of complex theories about "transubstantiation," and all sorts of rules about who can sit at the table and who can't. Imagine that! A closed guest list at a meal where the open-guest-list man of all time held forth. And this in the name of one who said that if important people had better things to do than attend the banquet of the kingdom, he'd drag in bums off the street to take their places.

It was just another lesson. The last one. The best one. We all have to eat, and eating in the ancient Near East was much more than a biological necessity. It was a social, political, and theological statement. It mattered very much who sat at your table, in what chair, and in what order. Shuffle the chairs, and change the occupants, and how was anybody going to know who was clean and unclean, who was wealthy, who was righteous?

It's been said that Jesus wasn't killed so much for the things he said as for the company he kept. His offense, according to Matthew, wasn't just that he hung out with sinners and tax collectors, but that "he *eats* with them!" The table wasn't just a flat spot for holding food; it was a diagram of decency, a line drawn in the sand, the last bastion of order and tradition for the people of God.

Things haven't really changed much. The table is still the last bastion of order and tradition in both family and society. Eating *still* isn't just a biological necessity—it's a spiritual exercise, and right down to the last detail, it's the most important barometer of the sacramental life. Just as the table holds the Church together, the table holds families together. Show me a family that doesn't eat a single daily meal together, and I'll show you a family that is passing itself in the hall.

In a recent issue of *The New Yorker*, Francine Du Plessix Gray lamented the depraved images of teenage life in the city of New York in a movie called *Kids*. One common thread in this disturbing portrait was that none of these children had ever been civilized by the ritual of a proper meal at home. She wrote: "This is not another pious harangue on 'spiritual starvation'; this is about the fact that we may be witnessing the first generation in history that has not been required to participate in that primal rite of socialization, the family meal."

Can anyone hones: ay that eating in one's car is an advance for civilization: ʌnd what about microwaves? They're great for reheating things, but were they supposed to replace the oven? Then there's the TV tray, which may be the ultimate blasphemy. It not only removes us from the table, but it turns us away from the faces we need to face!

For most of human history, people have scattered to *make a living*, and then huddled around a table to have a *life*. Through joy and sorrow they sat together—sometimes silently, sometimes with animated voices and boisterous laughter. But the making of a meal and the ritual of the table was the glue that stuck them together. Anyone who wishes to simplify her life, and to make sacramental moments out of ordinary time, cannot possibly ignore the function of the *table* as both an anchor and a conduit.

This then is part *one* of the *eleventh* prescription for a life grounded in the earth, but open to the possibility of heaven: put a heavy table in the center of your home, throw away the folding chairs, and stop thinking that you can always eat out and build a life within. Insist that those you love honor at least one mealtime a day; that you say grace, and say hello, and say something about the shape of the day. And don't start eating until everyone has been seated at the table.

Remember this: it is not just in the consumption of food that we have communion with one another, but in its preparation as well. Sadly, the rituals by which meals were once prepared, with someone chopping, and someone kneading, and someone uncorking and pouring the wine, are largely a thing of the past. Yet there is no lubricant to conversation like snapping beans or shucking corn, and there is no provocateur of the appetite like the aroma of food that is *becoming* a meal, but isn't yet. The catered lunch may be easier, but it ar-

rives without warning, and thus without much appeal, deny-
ing all the senses their principle pleasure: anticipation.

Part *two* of the *eleventh* prescription is aimed at those who
work with their heads, but seldom with their hands. The life
of the mind is a wonderful thing, but as one who lives it I can
assure you—it isn't enough. Ideas are powerful things, but
they are evanescent. Like sugar without protein, too much
thinking and not enough doing creates a sedentary illusion: I
think, therefore I have acted. Søren Kierkegaard tried to warn
us all about the dangerous illusion by which thinking good
thoughts is confused with the doing of good deeds. Like S.K.'s
famous parable "The Man Who Walked Backwards"—away
from you, while smiling and extending his hand as if to greet
you—the more good things we *talk* about doing, the less
obligation we feel to actually *do* them.

Witness the yuppies of my generation who believe that the
ultimate sign of having "made it" is to hire everything out.
Need a deck, hire someone to build it; need a garden, hire a
gardener; need to cut your lawn, that's what the neighbor boy
is for. White collar means clean hands. Success means working at concepts, pushing through components of the project
that someone else actually puts together. What gets lost in the
process is a connection to the physical world and to that soul-
fully satisfying thing we call "building it."

You may not think there's much you can do, but the truth
is, every trade can be learned, and nothing can take the place

of planning out a project, buying the materials, and doing the job yourself. You will make mistakes, of course, which is what keeps you humble. But you'll also discover that manipulating some small part of your world—changing it, re-creating it—satisfies at a very basic level. Forget your fingernails. Get to work.

Let's face it: we were not born with some sort of antiseptic, antimatter view of life. Children cover themselves in mud, they jump into puddles of rainwater, they smear food all over their faces. What's to say that adults should ever outgrow the need to get dirty? The smell of sawdust, and the feel of it clinging to your skin, is a simple pleasure. So is digging, so is cutting and gluing a pipe, so is turning a screw.

There has been many a morning before work, and many an evening after, when I was glad that nobody was checking up on me as I mumbled out my giddy delight over driving a bright silver nail into a freshly cut piece of wood that fit perfectly where it was supposed to go. Mixing up concrete is every bit as enjoyable as mixing up a cake, hosing down the deck is therapeutic, raking leaves in the fall can be glorious.

Just as we must stop segregating forms of work, and making those who *do* feel inferior to those who *plan,* we must also remember that physical labor is fundamentally a form of creativity. It may not be art, but at some level it requires imagination, aesthetic deliberation, and some kind of technique.

Brick masons take pride in what they do. So do plumbers. So do carpenters. Who's to say that what they do isn't art?

So in addition to returning to the table, it might also be wise to buy some tools. The simple life is a "hands-on" life, and the sacramental life sees beauty everywhere—even in the arc and click of a socket wrench, or the feathered sweep of a concrete trowel over a new set of steps. And yes, let your kids put their initials there! Let's banish forever the arrogance that regards labor as inferior to management, and pronounce all work holy again—lest we forget how things really get done.

XII

~~~~~~~

Waiting and Hoping: The Pleasure of Anticipation

"Hope" is the thing with feathers—
That perches in the soul—
And sings the tune without the words—
And never stops—at all—

—*Emily Dickinson*

Let's face it: patience as a virtue is long gone. We want everything in life right now, and regard waiting as a form of impotence. Instant gratification is the name of the game, from handsome starting salaries to cybersex to instant breakfast. There's no joy in the hunt, only in the catch, and if the catch takes too long, forget it.

Much modern technology is predicated on our desire to find a shortcut to everything: dating services promise to weed out undesirable traits, so we don't waste time learning things that are bound to disappoint us; condensed books promise all the plot with less verbal fat (who needs character development?); and shopping by phone after watching TV means that even the ancient and highly socialized art of barter can be a solitary exercise devoid of inconvenience and delay.

Our desire to have everything quickly has pushed child-hood so far back that it hardly exists anymore—innocence being one of those impractical stages that is ultimately a waste of time. Glamour Shots, for example, can take a twelve-year-old and make her look eighteen. Ellen Goodman has even suggested in a recent column that the real message of much political rhetoric these days is that childhood is simply too expensive and needs to be eliminated! For the rest of us, credit cards are the perfect symbol of the age—allowing us to have what we want *now*, and then worry about paying for it long after we have lost all enthusiasm for whatever it was we purchased.

The problem with all this goes beyond mere cynicism about the modern age. Philosophers and theologians have been trying for centuries to tell us what our lives can prove if only we will examine them: anticipation is not just a dependable pleasure in life, it may be the *principal* one. To look ahead to what might be, but isn't yet; to plan a way to change to-morrow; to hope for things yet to come, believing in possibility—these are things that sustain us when nothing else can.

One of the simple pleasures of the academic life is that every fall, in a ritual of renewal, students and professors flock to the bookstore—that symbol of possibility as real as the smell of fresh ink and binding glue. Every class has its required reading list: books students would never purchase if left to their own devices, and may not read if they can get away with it. But there they are: the seminal questions of Greek philosophers, the lyrical madness of poets, the wizards of science trying to measure the mystical—all in pursuit of the Holy Grail—wisdom.

In the fall, at the university, all things are possible. Every student may get an A, every lecture may be tipped with fire, every exam may probe the depths of meaning. It will not be that way, of course. But for one shining moment it *is* that way. It is that way in the bookstore, in the line at the cash register, under the spell of blank tablets, fresh markers, and backpacks full of possibility.

If ours is a civilization meant to survive, it will have to restore the ancient art of *hoping*. It will have to encourage the moral imagination, and nourish human dreams beyond those of private ambition. We need to be done with the illusion that good things can be had quickly, that saving money is old-fashioned, and that the finish line is the only part of the race that matters. Soul-making has its own schedule, so who are we to hurry things?

Life is a trip, not just a destination, and wisdom is born of longing. Just the same, our hopes need not be as remote as those of that memorable character in Dickens's *Bleak House*, Mrs. Jellyby, whose eyes are always cast far off, as if *they could see nothing nearer than Africa*. Many well-intentioned souls, aping her "telescopic philanthropy," are out to save the world, while under their noses there is neither joy nor well-tended children! We can hope for things close at hand: we can antic-ipate with pleasure the next meal, a good night's sleep, being with someone we love.

If you wish to elevate any conversation, ask your partner what he or she hopes to be someday. Living with tender hope is not a waste of time, and seeding life with possibility is not just the foolish sport of children. Living in the moment while anticipating the next may sound like a contradiction, but it is actually the unmistakable mark of the sacramental life.

This then is the *twelfth* and final prescription for a life that is simple without being simplistic, and sacramental without being doctrinaire: consider *hope* to be the one disposition for which there is no acceptable alternative. Be patient, and re-member how often things work out according to a wisdom that is beyond understanding. Along the way, don't ever give up the simple joy of looking forward to things that give you pleasure.

Life can be full of vain imaginings: the perfect spouse, the perfect child, the life of ease. These things are futile, and are not to be confused with hope as a religious idea. It is not per-fection, but peace of mind we seek; not perpetual happiness, but basic contentment; not a life of constant excitement, but of dependable satisfaction.

Do not look past the richness of so-called "ordinary mo-ments" in search of happiness on some distant shore. Put your oars in the water of *this* day, look after *this* hour and ask yourself what it means, and to whom it's important. Across the table from you sits someone looking for a word of encouragement, a smile, a reason to get up in the morning and to welcome the evening. At the first sign of trouble, we can't run from one another—it takes time to make a life. It takes patience. It takes a kind of sacramental hope.

Hold fast to precious memories and project them into the future, savoring the next time you might enjoy those moments again: a child against the cheek, the loyalty of a pet, the tenderness of a kiss, the aroma of a home-cooked meal, the bed of a lover, the trust of a little one, the satisfaction of work well done and a place to call home, the confidence of a coworker, an unexpected letter from a friend, ice cream on a long walk, early morning mist on the fishing pond, a phone call from someone you admire, the sound of a mountain stream, the boisterous laughter of children playing, the rhythmic glide of a rocking chair and the dragon-slaying sound of a lullaby, milk and cookies, a package in the mail, a surprise gift, fresh-cut flowers on the dinner table, the quiet beckoning of a bookmark, the smell of a new bar of soap, the feel of an ironed shirt and a comfortable pair of shoes.

The life of simple pleasures is a state of mind, as much as a state of being. It's a meeting of soul and sensation, available to everyone, guaranteed to no one. But this much is certain: life is amazing if one is paying attention. There is hatred and cruelty to be sure, but there is also beauty and truth—cells that differentiate, moons that rise, and water that floats up from the sea to fall as rain and then runs to the sea again.

The days given to us are few, and they race away like low clouds pushed by a storm. The moments we have are brief, like puppies spilled from a cardboard box; they tumble over one another, squealing, and then they're gone. The bright morning of innocence gives way to the hard work of midday, then to the pensiveness of late afternoon, then to the lengthening shadows of evening, and then to the Long Sleep from which there is no waking.

The Kingdom of Heaven is within us, and about us, but we can see it only with the eyes of the heart. When we walk into it for one instant, one luminescent moment, we have a working definition of eternity.

In the meantime (which W. H. Auden reminded us is the only time we have), try these twelve things: Renew the lost art of *conversation*, for without talk life is a silent misunderstanding. Go to concerts and listen to live *music*, for without rhythm life is little more than respiration. Never stop eating *books*, for they are the feast of the imagination. And those of you with children, remember that *parenting* is a kind of twenty-four-hour-a-day domestic religion, with the Little gods always watching.

Be kind to *four-legged ones* and all the creatures of the earth as if your humanity depended on it, because it does. Consider writing a letter or bringing a thoughtful gift, for there is no grace above *consideration*. Remember that "Carpe Diem" is more than a slogan on a T-shirt; it's a way of life that *seizes the moment*. Put the kiss back in the kitchen, and return *romance* to the Temple where it belongs.

Throw away any religion that circles the wagons and makes you meaner, and replace it with one that makes you more *merciful*. Remember that *freedom* has nothing to do with how much you can get away with, and everything to do with the indebtedness you choose on behalf of others. Get out of the drive-through lane and into the recipe box or the toolbox, because *cooking something* and *building something* are good for you. And finally, be patient as the world unfolds. *Anticipation* can cover the short run, and *hope* can cover the rest.

DR. ROBIN R. MEYERS is a senior minister of the Mayflower Congregational Church in Oklahoma City, and a professor of speech and rhetoric at Oklahoma City University. He has been a regular editorial commentator for National Public Radio. Robin lives in Oklahoma City with his wife, a sculptor, and their three children.